The Voices Of Christmas

Readers' Theater For Advent

Jerry Nordstrom

CSS Publishing Company, Inc., Lima, Ohio

THE VOICES OF CHRISTMAS

Copyright © 1996 by
CSS Publishing Company, Inc.
Lima, Ohio

The original purchaser may photocopy material in this publication for use as it was intended (i.e. worship material for worship use; educational material for classroom use; dramatic material for staging or production). No additional permission is required from the publisher for such copying by the original purchaser only. Inquiries should be addressed to: Permissions, CSS Publishing Company, Inc., P.O. Box 4503, Lima, Ohio 45802-4503.

Some scripture quotations are from the *New Revised Standard Version of the Bible*, copyright 1989 by the Division of Christian Education of the National Council of the Churches of Christ in the USA. Used by permission.

Some scripture quotations are from the *Revised Standard Version of the Bible*, copyrighted 1946, 1952 ©, 1971, 1973, by the Division of Christian Education of the National Council of the Churches of Christ in the USA. Used by permission.

Some scripture quotations are from the *King James Version of the Bible*, in the public domain.

ISBN 0-7880-0837-4   PRINTED IN U.S.A.

This work is dedicated to all those who, in preparing for Christmas, have sometimes lost the joy and meaning of it.

The Voices Of Christmas

Cast

PATIENT — Resident of a nursing home (male)

HOMEMAKER — Food-happy matron (female)

SHOPPER — Wealthy, materialistic socialite (female)

SPORTSMAN — Young ski enthusiast (male)

MERCHANT — Toy store owner (male)

TRADITIONALIST — Sentimental Swedish-American grandma (female)

CORPORATION MAN — Heavy-drinking party-goer (male)

*CHILD — Greedy little girl (female)

WORKING WIFE — Frazzled victim of the Christmas rush (female)

*May be read, in character, by an adult.

Presentation time: about half an hour

Using irony and humor, this work is designed to reveal the realities of Christmas — both the detrimental and the divine. This is not a play with scenery and characters who speak to one another. Cast members address visualized listeners as if no interruptions from other characters or changes of subject occur. Lines may be read or recited; most important is that lines sound spontaneous and real. The cast may stand or be seated on various levels. No one needs to move about, though a limited amount of pantomime is recommended. During telephone calls, listening time should be allowed where there are dashes. A few identifying, symbolic items of costume or props may be used, if they are not distracting. If any element in the script is seen as outmoded, it may be updated.

The Voices Of Christmas

(The first lines may be said over the fading, recorded strains of "Jingle Bells.")

PATIENT: Christmas must be coming up. It's on TV quite a lot — the commercials, you know.

HOMEMAKER: I've got a pretty good start on my Christmas baking. I just love this time of year.

SHOPPER: I just don't know what to buy the Whittiers — not that I don't have any ideas; it's just a matter of deciding.

MERCHANT: Christmas is coming and, as owner of the Santa Land Discount Toy and Candy Store, I couldn't be happier.

TRADITIONALIST: My little granddaughter was chosen to be Lucia at a Sancta Lucia Fest this year. Sweetest thing you ever saw. Henry and I flew out just to see her.
[Swedes celebrate December 13 in honor of Lucia (pronounced Loos-EE-ah), the Sicilian saint who, according to tradition, was seen radiating light and bringing food to the starving in medieval Sweden. Today, eldest daughters or specially chosen young women wear lighted crowns and carry breakfast to their families or wherever festivities are held.]

CORPORATION MAN: We had our office party already. What a blast!

CHILD: Mommy took me to see Santy Claus! I gave him my list.

WORKING WIFE: Next year, I swear, I'm going to do my Christmas shopping in July.

CORPORATION MAN: You should have heard my boss joking and laughing at that party — he does it only once a year.

TRADITIONALIST: I thought my son-in-law was going to have a fit about those lighted candles in the Lucia crown, so we covered her head with aluminum foil.

SHOPPER: Last year the Whittiers gave us those lovely Waterford crystal egg cups and Tiffany spoons.

MERCHANT: We have a complete line of every toy and candy a kid could want — even more than last year, and last year we really made a killing.

SPORTSMAN: For Christmas I want snow!

CHILD: I want a Barbie doll.

HOMEMAKER: I already have twelve yummy kinds of cookies baked ...

CHILD: And a Ken doll.

HOMEMAKER: A double batch of each ...

CHILD: And complete Barbie and Ken wardrobes.

HOMEMAKER: Besides what I have in the freezer, of course.

PATIENT: There was a group of carolers down the hall a few days ago.

WORKING WIFE: I don't know. I'm so tired when I get home. I should have written the cards on Halloween.

TRADITIONALIST: I suppose it is a silly custom, but — no, it isn't! It's a beautiful tradition, and I don't think we should change a thing. We need to maintain our traditions.

SPORTSMAN: We're driving out on the 24th. Me and these other two guys. We wanna have, ya know, four full days of skiing.

TRADITIONALIST: I think traditions are very important, don't you?

PATIENT: They say Christmas trees are a fire hazard here.

WORKING WIFE: What I want to know is: Why do we always wait for the coldest day of the year to buy a tree?

CHILD: And I want a doll house with four floors.

CORPORATION MAN: We've got this secretary who always gets so bombed!

SHOPPER: I thought we might get them individual, jade, mint-jelly cups ...

CHID: I want some white mice.

SHOPPER: But they already have them.

HOMEMAKER: Did you see those cookies that Irma served? Of course, she bought them.

MERCHANT: It's a cutthroat operation, this toy business; the competition is really tough. Believe me, if it weren't for Christmas I wouldn't be in this racket.

TRADITIONALIST: I've given Advent calendars to each of my grandchildren, all different. The cutest things!

WORKING WIFE: I asked my husband to bring home some wrapping paper. You should have seen what he brought! Aqua and yellow-green Christmas balls on a bright green background. I think I married Mr. Yuck!

HOMEMAKER: I made my nephew some strawberry cookies. I think he'll get a kick out of it because I threw in a few that look just like blueberries, too.

SHOPPER: I looked at some pearl-handled oyster forks, but they only had thirteen in stock.

PATIENT: The sun hasn't been shining much lately, has it?

CORPORATION MAN: It's just a good thing they don't invite families to these office parties or there wouldn't be a marriage left by Christmas. I mean, WOW!

CHILD: My grandpa promised me a real, live puppy dog for Christmas.

TRADITIONALIST: I'm having the girls over, and we're going to string popcorn and cranberries. Won't that be fun?

WORKING WIFE: I can't help it that we exchange presents with more of my relatives than his.

CHILD: And I want some goldfish.

WORKING WIFE: If he thinks I'm going to cross off my uncle and aunt in Peoria just because he's never met them, he's got another think coming!

PATIENT: My roommate had some company this week. They said it'd been pretty slippery driving.

WORKING WIFE: What am I supposed to do, exterminate seven of my nine nieces and nephews just because he's only got two?

CHILD: And I want a two-wheeler.

MERCHANT: This year I expect to get pretty far with the Evel Knievel Risk-Your-Life kit.

SPORTSMAN: When we get back, we're planning to go snowmobiling New Year's Day but, ya know, not real early.

TRADITIONALIST: My son-in-law hates it, but maybe if I start them young enough, the grandchildren will learn to like lutefisk. *[pronounced LUU-te-fisk]*

HOMEMAKER: Our circle packed cheer boxes for shut-ins Tuesday morning. I brought cookies — five kinds. It's a good thing, too. No one else had thought to bring anything good for *us* to eat.

TRADITIONALIST: I was so upset with the Sunday School program this year. The children sang, and that was nice, but they didn't have any of the little tots saying pieces or anything like they used to. You know how adorable those little tykes are when they get up there. Such a shame. I mean, what is Christmas for if it's not for the children?

CHILD: And I want a new color TV — and a VCR ...

CORPORATION MAN: You've seen in the movies where the uptight career girl takes off her glasses and lets her hair down? We had one like that at our office party!

HOMEMAKER: I baked a coffee ring. It turned out so pretty I wanted to hang it on the door for a wreath.

CORPORATION MAN: You shoulda seen the boss chasin' her around the desks. Knocked over the Christmas tree and two plastic palms. Wild!

SPORTSMAN: Next Christmas I'm going to Switzerland!

CHILD: And I want a pair of skis.

SPORTSMAN: Yeah, it makes my folks sore, ya know, when I'm gone at Christmas time, but, man! When I've got a week off, I mean, I've got to ski!

PATIENT: I used to get cards from my sister's family in Ohio, but I lost track of them some years ago.

TRADITIONALIST: I just don't understand people rushing off to Florida or Mexico at Christmastime! I think it's terrible. I don't know how anybody could have the Christmas spirit under a palm tree! Christmas must not mean much to some people. It's sad, really.

SHOPPER: I thought about buying the Whittiers table linen, but the only thing worth buying costs over $400, and I'm not sure they've ever spent that much on us.

MERCHANT: Maybe if that Middle East situation flares up again we could unload some of those war toys. There isn't enough real war news to get the kids excited right now. Too bad. We've got a big stock.

WORKING WIFE: My husband's parents are just impossible to buy for.

CHILD: And, of course, I want furniture for my doll house.

WORKING WIFE: Why *I* should have to do all the shopping for *his* relatives, I'll never know.

HOMEMAKER: I don't know what happened last year; so few showed up for our Christmas Day open house. Some said they didn't know about it, but the invitation was clearly printed in our four-page Christmas letter.

MERCHANT: Gun sales aren't quite what they should be either. I blame those bleeding-heart liberals in the news media. People get shot, and right away *(shaking head in disbelief)* they're cryin' about guns! I don't know.

PATIENT: The nurses have been putting up some Christmas decorations. I almost wish they wouldn't.

CORPORATION MAN: This guy in my office is having a big bash on Christmas Eve. The wife says she'll go only if *I* find the baby-sitter! Now, that's real Christmas spirit for you.

WORKING WIFE: I have this dreadful feeling that I've forgotten to buy for someone.

HOMEMAKER: I've ordered this thirty-pound turkey, so together with the ham and beef tenderloin ...

SPORTSMAN: We're staying in this friend's condo. And once we get to the chalet, we expect to make some friends, you know what I mean? It'll be a merry Christmas!

SHOPPER: A set of sterling silver pimento forks might be nice.

CHILD: And I want a real fur coat. A red one.

TRADITIONALIST: John, my son-in-law, isn't too keen on Scandinavian foods and things, but I think it would be nice to show the children a real Swedish Christmas, don't you?

HOMEMAKER: You should see the lovely Christmas tree skirt I've made! It's decorated with candy canes and holly. And I've just finished two dozen new tree ornaments: styrofoam balls covered with artificial fruit.

WORKING WIFE: What do you mean, "That isn't a nice enough gift for your mother?" It cost $12 more than I spent on my mother's present!

CHILD: And I want ice skates.

WORKING WIFE: If you don't like it, why don't *you* do the Christmas shopping? She's *your* mother, you know.

CORPORATION MAN: *(On phone)* Hello, Linda? This is Paul Martin. You know, down the block? — Tommy's dad. — Ah, we were wondering if you could sit with Tommy Monday the 24th. — Ah, yeah, that is Christmas Eve. — Oh. — Well, thanks anyway. — Yeah, sure, maybe some other time.

WORKING WIFE: I get home from work at six, I fix your supper, I wash your dishes, wash your clothes, clean the house, and I've got all these thousands of packages to wrap. I don't see why you can't at least help address a few of these stupid cards!

CHILD: And I want a magic kit.

SHOPPER: Be a darling and book me a morning flight to New York. I have some last minute shopping to do.

PATIENT: I've got a lot of memories but not many friends any more.

SPORTSMAN: I don't know what to do about presents, ya know, for my folks.

MERCHANT: We have a number of adult games for sale, too. One that's moving especially well is the godfather game, Make Me an Offer.

HOMEMAKER: This year I'm giving everyone red and green cross-stitched aprons with Christmas recipe cards in the pockets.

TRADITIONALIST: I've been calling all around, but I can't find a church with a 5 a.m. Swedish Julota *[pronounced JUUL-o-tah]* service on Christmas morning! Every year it gets harder and harder.

SPORTSMAN: I looked at some sweaters when I picked up my new ski boots, but I can't quite see my mother in a $150 ski sweater!

CORPORATION MAN: *(On phone)* Hello, Jennifer? This is Paul Martin — you know, over on Duxbury Drive? — Well, anyway, Sally said that — Sally Harrison. She said she thought you might be free to baby-sit Monday night. — Yes, the 24th. — Yes, I know that's Christmas Eve! — Well! A very merry Christmas to you, too! What a ....

CHILD: And I want a panda bear big enough to sit on.

CORPORATION MAN: Trouble is kids have too much money these days. Offer 'em a chance to *earn* a little money and they're insulted!

SPORTSMAN: I wonder about a pair of gloves for Mom. I don't mean ski gloves; I mean something she can wear, ya know, when she's shoveling snow.

WORKING WIFE: Oh! This house is a mess! There isn't a flat surface left anywhere! Maybe if I were one of those housewives who stayed home all day, I could bake and clean and have a pretty house for Christmas, too!

SHOPPER: What do you mean they're fully booked? Did you tell them who I am?

CHILD: And I want a bracelet and a ring and a necklace and a ...

SHOPPER: No, I do not want coach! You know I can't stand anything but first-class! Give me that phone! *(On phone)* This is Buffy Bufforpington!

SPORTSMAN: I wonder if I could get my mother's VISA card?

WORKING WIFE: No, I can't! I'm too busy! Why don't you learn to iron your own ugly, old bowling shirt?

CORPORATION MAN: *(On phone)* Well, yes, Mrs. Simpson, I know that's Christmas Eve. I just thought she might. — You see it's a family emergency, and, ah — well, I'm, I'm, I'm sorry I called your daughter, a, ah, ah, that name, but she — ah, yeah, but you see, she, ah, she ...

HOMEMAKER: Tomorrow I think I'll make a double batch of gingerbread men.

MERCHANT: I just signed this TV contract. From now until Christmas, a commercial for Santa Land Discount Toy and Candy Store will interrupt every Saturday morning cartoon at least twelve times.

PATIENT: I remember when I had my own home how we would have a tree and usually a nice chicken dinner. When I was a child, my mother always fixed a goose for Christmas dinner.

TRADITIONALIST: I have been all over this town looking for fresh lingonberries. I'm getting worried!

CORPORATION MAN: Listen, in a town this size there's got to be somebody who isn't all tied up just because it's Christmas Eve! Now think!

PATIENT: I wonder if anybody ever fixes goose anymore? They'll give us turkey here, I suppose. We get it about once a week anyhow. A lot cheaper than beef, I guess.

SHOPPER: *(On phone)* Well! I don't see why I should *have* to make reservations in advance, after all — Yes, I know it's Christmas! That's why I need to get to New York!

CHILD: And I want a trip to Disneyland.

SHOPPER: *(On phone)* All right then! If you insist on being difficult, you can get me a flight to San Francisco leaving tomorrow morning and returning the following morning. — *Yes,* first class! And I want a suite and dinner reservations at the St. Francis. And I think you should know, Mr. Smith, unless you start delivering better service, I may be using another travel agency in the future.

CHILD: And to Disneyworld.

SPORTSMAN: I could get my dad a box of cigars. But he doesn't smoke.

WORKING WIFE: I don't know what I'm going to do! Don's old army buddy is arriving *tomorrow* so he can spend *Christmas* with us! He just writes on the bottom of a Christmas card that he's coming! We only got the card today! And what's more, he's bringing his girlfriend!

CORPORATION MAN: Maybe he's old enough to stay alone.

HOMEMAKER: Did you notice how Madge hinted around for my caramel Christmas nut ball recipe? She'll never get it.

SPORTSMAN: I guess I'll get him a tie.

CHILD: And I want a nutcracker music box.

SPORTSMAN: I'm just glad my parents didn't make me wait until Christmas to give me the money for my new ski boots.

WORKING WIFE: No. I'm not wrapping one more present, and I'm not tying one more bow. And if you think I'm going out shopping for that bum and his girlfriend, you can forget it! Nobody invited them here in the first place, and — You *what?*

CORPORATION MAN: I wonder if anyone has ever thought of calling for a sitter at the Old Soldiers' Home?

MERCHANT: We're running low on bulletproof jackets, size 4.

SHOPPER: *(On phone)* Hello, dear, I've decided to pick up a few last-minute things in San Francisco tomorrow. I was wondering if you would be an angel and transfer about $4,000 to my account. That awful bank called me again this morning. I do wish you would speak to them about that.

CHILD: And I want a backyard cable car.

SPORTSMAN: The money didn't quite buy the boots I wanted, but, well, maybe someday, ya know.

TRADITIONALIST: I got the best idea for place cards! At each plate I'm putting a little straw goat with a card in his mouth! Just adorable!

PATIENT: When I was a child, we didn't have money for Christmas presents much. Maybe an orange or an apple. Sometimes a bag of candy.

CHILD: And I want all the newest video games.

SPORTSMAN: Maybe I could get Sis a pair of earrings. Man! That sure is a neat sweater she's knitting for me!

HOMEMAKER: I can't decide between plum pudding and pumpkin pie — or maybe brandied mince with hard sauce.

PATIENT: Someone came by here and passed out little bags of candy the other day.

HOMEMAKER: Maybe I should just make some of each.

MERCHANT: Call a meeting of all employees! Deny everything! Tell 'em we'll fire and sue anybody that leaks information about poisonous snakes found in that shipment of dolls from Taiwan! That's one kind of publicity we don't want!

CHILD: And I want a reptile garden.

WORKING WIFE: I know we're overdrawn, but we've got to eat! And you know who invited two more mouths to feed.

CORPORATION MAN: *(On phone)* Hello, dear. Yeah, it's me. Ah, sorry not to call you earlier — Ah, yeah, sorry about dinner but you see, I'm, I'm, ah, in, ah, well, some of us from the office stopped for a little happy hour and, ah, I ah — I'm sorry, honey. — I know I promised. — Ah, no-o, I don't think so. I, ah, I'm in jail. — Two weeks. Better call and cancel that guy at the Old Soldiers' Home. — But, this is the only call I can make, so could you call 'em at work? And tell your folks I'm sorry about Christmas Day. — Just make up something! Tell Tommy, ah, tell Tommy — No! *Please* don't! Tell him, tell him I'm away on business.

PATIENT: As a child, I remember we used to hitch up the team to the bobsled — we didn't have a sleigh, but we had sleigh bells! My dad would bundle us kids up in a big buffalo robe. We always went to church on Christmas.

TRADITIONALIST: *(On phone)* Well! Hello, dear! Such a nice surprise! I didn't think we'd hear from you till we saw you! How nice of you to call! *(Singing)* "It's beginning to look a lot like Christmas!" — What's that, dear? — John is taking off a whole week! How wonderful! — What? — You're not ... Henry! Henry! Turn off that TV! Christine is on the phone; she says John insists on taking the family to Cancun for Christmas! *(Beginning to wail)* Oh, Henry, they're not coming!

SHOPPER: *(On phone)* Hello, dear. Surprise, surprise: I'm in Kansas City. Some problem about weather after leaving San Francisco. I've called the Pilfertons, and Marguerite was so sweet. She's sending someone to pick me up, and she's talked me into going to their Christmas ball tonight. Of course, I'm here without a thing to wear, but if I hurry, I should be able to pick up something. The thing is, I seem to have left home without my American Express card, and I know it's hard to believe, but I've hit the max on the VISA and Master Cards I have with me, so I was wondering if you would be an angel and put some money in my checking account. Three or four thousand ought to do. That's a dear. I'll be home for sure on the 24th. Tell Martha to set for fourteen, and tell her I've decided on the pheasant.

CHILD: And I want a virtual reality machine.

PATIENT: Last year I tried to watch a church service on television on Christmas Eve. But I went to bed. It's not the same.

MERCHANT: *(On phone)* You have got to suppress that news item! The snakes haven't bitten anybody. It's no big deal! Just remember that I have a sizeable contract with you people. — Yes, forty commercials every Saturday morning! — The public does *not* have the right to know! *(Shifting tactics)* How about if we expand that commercial coverage to every afternoon from two to six? — Mr. Pierce! "Bribe?" How can you say such a thing?

HOMEMAKER: *(Feebly)* Everett, you'll just have to call up everybody and tell them not to come, that's all. I just cannot cook a sit-down dinner for twelve with the stomach flu!

WORKING WIFE: Donald, I'm sorry! But I refuse to have that woman in my house, and he's no better. I can't take it any more! I don't care if he did save your life in Vietnam. It's either them or me! Either they go or I go!

SPORTSMAN: *(On phone)* Hello, Mom? — Oh, yeah, Merry Christmas. I've got some bad news: I broke my leg.

SHOPPER: *(On phone)* Hello, Martha! Tell my husband when he arrives at home that I am in serious trouble. I am snowbound in Des Moines, Iowa! And the airline has lost *all* my luggage! It's just incredible! Tell him he has to do something about getting me out of here! It's just too terrible! — No, you go right ahead with our plans for dinner tonight, except, I've decided against the pheasant. I want filet of reindeer.

PATIENT: There's a bunch of young people singing "Jingle Bells" down the hall. I'm sure they mean well.

TRADITIONALIST: Oh, that dreadful John! How could he do such a dreadful thing? When I think of all the trouble I've gone to ...

CHILD: Mommy! Mommy! Jody says there *isn't* any Santy Claus!

(After the following nine lines have been said in sequence, they will be repeated over and over, on top of one another, with ever-increasing volume until a chime is loudly sounded.)

WORKING WIFE: This is too much to take!

MERCHANT: I'm ruined! Bankrupt!

TRADITIONALIST: I've never been so disappointed in my life!

SHOPPER: I insist that you get me out of here!

PATIENT: Christmas is the loneliest time of the year.

HOMEMAKER: I could just die!

SPORTSMAN: I don't know what I'm going to do.

CORPORATION MAN: I still can't believe it.

CHILD: It's a lie! A mean, horrible lie!

(When the repetition and the volume of these nine lines has grown gradually until nearly deafening, a loud, clear, single, resonant chime cuts through the din. All voices stop very suddenly, and

during a lengthy pause, all that is heard is the reverberation of the chime. To achieve this, a triangle, bell, circular saw blade, or a resonant pipe or tube may be firmly struck.

At this point, if props or symbolic items of costuming have been used, they can be set side. Soft, ethereal music may be introduced and used as background to the following lines, each of which is to be said — in contrast to the former — as an eager expression of good news.)

TRADITIONALIST: Be not afraid; for behold, I bring you good news of a great joy which will come to all people.

PATIENT: The wilderness and the dry land shall be glad; and the desert shall rejoice, and blossom as the rose.

CHILD: For unto us a child is born, unto us a son is given.

MERCHANT: And you shall call his name Jesus for it is he that shall save his people from their sins.

CORPORATION MAN: For God so loved the world, that he gave his only begotten Son.

SPORTSMAN: In him was life, and the life was the light of all.

WORKING WIFE: The light shines in the darkness and the darkness has not overcome it.

CORPORATION MAN: That whosoever believes in him should not perish, but have everlasting life.

SHOPPER: Everyone that thirsts, come to the waters.

SPORTSMAN: Listen, and your soul will live.

TRADITIONALIST: For to you is born this day in the city of David a Savior who is Christ the Lord.

CHILD: And his name shall be called Wonderful Counselor,

MERCHANT: Mighty God,

PATIENT: Everlasting Father,

SHOPPER: Prince of Peace.

ALL: Glory to God in the highest and on earth peace among those with whom he is pleased!

[An appropriate conclusion would be to segue into the singing of "Come, Thou Dear Redeemer," music by Cesar Franck, words adapted from a hymn by Charles Wesley, and published in Solos for the Church Year: A Collection of Sacred Songs, *by Lawson-Gould Music Publishers, Inc., N.Y.; G. Schirmer, Inc., sole selling representative, N.Y.]*